This book is dedicated to all the Mamas who always read *just one more*.

Jordan Linzy Morgan

A Tennessee wife and mom, Jordan has a passion for words and bringing families together through books. She is a lover of storytelling, authentic motherhood, and always making the time to slow down and take a swing on the front porch.

www.jordanmorgan.com

Michelle Kiely

A local artist from Knoxville, Michelle specializes in large-scale murals, but enjoys painting with watercolors and other mediums. A lover of all things outdoors, she enjoys spending time with her husband and children at all of the wonderful places East Tennessee has to offer.

www.muralsbymichelle.com

Art Alley has many wonderful colors.

Everyone here loves a Bluetick.

You can put your toes in sand at The Cove.

Downtown is a neat place to go!

East Tennessee is where we call home.

Friends are easy to find here.
Just say hello!

On **G**ame days, we wear orange and white.

Henley Street Bridge is beautiful at night.

Ijams Nature Center has critters galore.

Do you know a good place to **J**ump in the lake?

Knoxville is a great place to be.

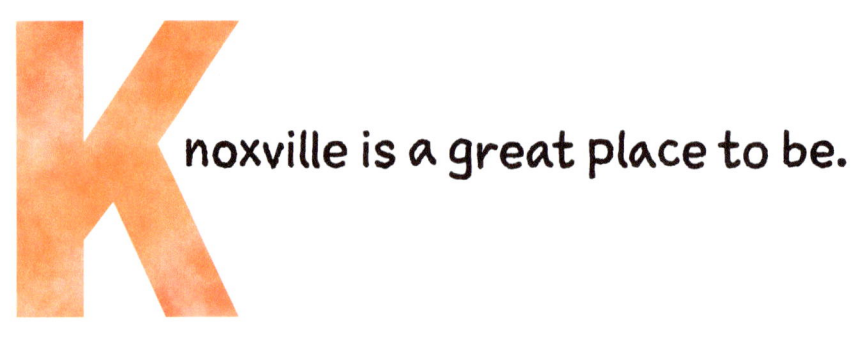

We **L**ove our southern town.

Market Square has something for everyone!

N eyland is busy on Saturday.

The **O**ld City is full of history.

Quarries can be a cool place to swim.

The Tennessee River winds through the city.

The Sunsphere is a skyline staple.

The ennessee Theatre has a sign that shines!

Underground you'll find the Cherokee Caverns.

Everyone here is a **V**olunteer.

World's Fair Park is lots of fun.

X marks the spot of Knoxville on a map.

Y 'all can be heard everywhere you go.

We all enjoy a quick trip to the Zoo.

Now YOU can find all of these letters in Knoxville!

Text copyright © 2024 by Jordan Linzy Morgan.

Illustrations copyright © 2024 by Michelle Kiely.

All rights reserved.

No portion of this book may be reproduced in any form without written permission from the publisher, illustrator, or author, except as permitted by U.S. copyright law.

ISBNs

Hardcover: 979-8-9888724-0-5
Paperback: 979-8-9888724-1-2
Ebook: 979-8-9888724-2-9

For further contact: P.O. Box 131 Walland, TN 37886

www.ingramcontent.com/pod-product-compliance
Lightning Source LLC
Chambersburg PA
CBHW051513110526
44582CB00008B/148